Cornerstones of Freedom

The Battle for Iwo Jima

TOM McGOWEN

CHILDREN'S PRESS®
A Division of Grolier Publishing
New York • London • Hong Kong • Sydney
Danbury, Connecticut

Visit Children's Press on the Internet at:
http://publishing.grolier.com

Library of Congress Cataloging-in-Publication Data

McGowen, Tom.
  The battle for Iwo Jima / Tom McGowen.
    p. cm.—(Cornerstones of freedom)
  Includes index.
  Summary: Relates the events preceding, during, and after the battle for
the tiny Japanese island of Iwo Jima, where American victory hastened the
end of World War II.
  ISBN: 0-516-21141-2 (lib. bdg.)   0-516-26458-3 (pbk.)
  1. Iwo Jima, Battle of, 1945—Juvenile literature. [1. Iwo Jima, Battle of,
1945. 2. World War, 1939–1945—Campaigns.] I. Title. II. Series.
D767.99.I9M33   1999
340.54`26—dc21
                                                                98–3491
                                                                    CIP
                                                                    AC

As the year 1945 began, most Americans had never heard of a place called Iwo Jima. Iwo Jima is a tiny island in the Pacific Ocean, only about 5 miles (8 kilometers) long and 3 miles (5 km) wide. Located about 750 miles (1,200 km) south of Japan, its name means "Sulfur Island" in Japanese. The island is formed entirely of black volcanic rock. At its tip rises Mount Suribachi, a 550-foot (152-meter)-high extinct volcano. The beaches that run along parts of the island are coarse black volcanic sand. In 1945, there were only a few small trees and bushes dotting the landscape. Iwo Jima was a small, dark, ugly place that stank of sulfur—a smell similar to rotten eggs. And in 1945, it became an important part of United States history.

Iwo Jima's location south of Japan made it a target for battle during World War II.

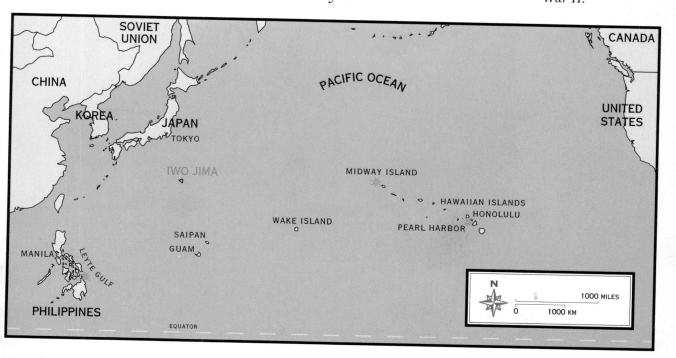

At that time, the United States was fighting in World War II (1939–45). For the United States, the war had begun about three years earlier. On December 7, 1941, Japanese warplanes made a sneak bombing attack on the U.S. naval base at Pearl Harbor, Hawaii. Ships of the U.S. Pacific Fleet were caught by surprise and badly damaged. Japan then launched a series of attacks against other American bases in the Pacific Ocean, capturing Wake Island, the Philippine Islands, and Guam. Japan's allies, Germany and Italy, also declared war on the United States.

Thick smoke rolls from two American battleships, the USS *West Virginia (foreground) and the* USS *Tennessee (background) following the Japanese attack on Pearl Harbor, Hawaii, on December 7, 1941.*

Although this Japanese aircraft carrier stationed in the Pacific Ocean has been damaged by enemy gunfire, it was difficult to gain any real advantage over the Japanese for months after Pearl Harbor.

For a while, it seemed that the entire Pacific Ocean was controlled by the Japanese navy, which was much bigger than what was left of the U.S. Pacific Fleet. Japan had twice as many battleships and aircraft carriers, and many more cruisers and destroyers. Most of the islands in the Pacific were Japanese bases where ships of the Japanese navy could go for supplies, fuel, and repairs. The United States had few such bases. As a result, American commanders devised a plan to defeat Japan by attacking and capturing its island bases. Then, U.S. forces would be able to use the captured bases to launch attacks on Japan and conquer it.

By the beginning of 1945, most of the American plan had been victoriously carried out. The U.S. Navy had crippled the Japanese fleet in the Battle of Midway (June 4–6, 1942) northwest of the Hawaiian Islands, and had nearly destroyed it in the Battle for Leyte Gulf (October 23–26, 1944) in the Philippines. Most of Japan's island bases also had been captured. American B-29 bombers could fly from airfields on islands near Japan, inflicting damage on Japanese cities and industries. The damage made the plan to invade Japan easier because the country would be unable to fight back.

But there was one problem. A little group of Japanese-controlled islands still lay between

This photograph is an aerial view of Iwo Jima. Mount Suribachi is in the lower right corner. The two sets of strips in the middle of the island are airfields.

American forces and Japan. Iwo Jima was one of those islands, and American bombers heading for Japan had to fly right over it. From airfields on Iwo Jima, Japanese planes attacked the bombers as they passed. Radio messages were sent quickly to

An American B-29 bomber on a bombing raid over Japanese islands in the Pacific Ocean in 1944

Japan, warning that U.S. bombers were approaching. This gave the Japanese time to prepare their planes and antiaircraft guns to fight the Americans. As a result, the American bombers were suffering serious losses. American commanders decided to attack and capture Iwo Jima. This would not only make bomber flights safer, but would also give American forces new airfields that were closer to Japan. The island could also be used as a base for the invasion of Japan.

The Japanese commanders were also aware of Iwo Jima's strategic location. They had expected an attack on the island and were prepared for it.

Japanese troops in the Pacific were confident they would be victorious in the war.

Iwo Jima was defended by about twenty-two thousand Japanese troops, under the command of Lieutenant General Tadamichi Kuribayashi, who made the island into one big fortress. Deep underground caves were widened, reinforced with concrete, and turned into shelters. Once inside these shelters, Japanese troops could safely wait out air raids or bombardments by the giant guns of American battleships. Hollow domes of thick concrete, built to stop bullets and to withstand explosions, were constructed all over the island. These domes were called gun emplacements, and cannons, machine guns, and antitank guns were placed inside. The gun emplacements were camouflaged (disguised) to look like natural bumps and ridges in the ground, becoming easy for an enemy to overlook. Hundreds of land mines that would explode instantly if stepped on were buried in the ground around them. Many large cannons were hidden on the slopes of Mount Suribachi. From the volcano's flat top, observers could see every part of the island and tell the cannon crews where to fire. With all of these defenses, there would not be any place where invading enemy troops could be safe.

Kuribayashi, however, did not think he could prevent the Americans from capturing the island. But even if he couldn't, he did not intend to surrender. He encouraged his troops to make the invasion as difficult for the Americans as possible. He asked his soldiers to vow that they would each try to kill at least ten Americans before they themselves were killed.

The Third, Fourth, and Fifth Divisions of the United States Marine Corps were selected to carry out the invasion of Iwo Jima. A division was made up of about twenty thousand men (at that time, there were no women in a marine division), with twenty-four large cannons, and a variety of other weapons, including tanks. The heart of a division consisted of three regiments of troops on foot. There were about three thousand men in a regiment. These were the men who would fight the Japanese in close combat, killing or capturing as many of them as possible until the battle was won. Most of these marines used the Garand rifle, which could fire eight shots before being reloaded. Some men fought with machine guns, others carried flamethrowers, machines with nozzles that sprayed burning streams of liquid. Still others operated small cannons called mortars.

U.S. Navy Vice Admiral Richmond Turner commanded both the marine and navy forces that would invade Iwo Jima. Turner's nickname was "Terrible Turner" because of his hot temper. Major General Harry Schmidt, nicknamed "the Dutchman," would command the marine invasion.

The American commanders knew that Iwo Jima had strong defenses. They decided first to weaken these defenses in preparation for the invasion. On December 8, 1944, U.S. Army Air Corps planes began bombing raids on the island almost every day. Some days, American warships off Iwo Jima would fire on the island for hours at a time. These bombing raids and bombardments took place throughout December 1944, and into January and February 1945.

The invasion of Iwo Jima required hundreds of ships of all kinds. These are troop carriers headed for the shore.

But they actually did little damage to the Japanese defenses. Safe in the underground caves, the Japanese soldiers waited through the hours of explosions that shook the island. Afterward, any damage to gun emplacements or airfields was quickly repaired.

On February 14, 1945, a huge American invasion fleet of hundreds of ships sailed for Iwo Jima from the island of Saipan, which is located about 600 miles (966 km) from Iwo Jima. Other ships sailed from the island of Guam, and dozens of warships also joined the fleet. As the sun rose on the morning of February 16, the Japanese on Iwo Jima saw that the island was surrounded by American warships. Shortly after, a three-day pounding of the island began. The big guns of six battleships and several smaller ships all fired at carefully selected places. Airplanes from the invasion fleet's aircraft carriers swooped down over the island, dropping high-explosive bombs and flaming napalm (jellylike gasoline that can burn a large area). A U.S. Navy Underwater Demolition Team, known as "frogmen," planted explosives to destroy the underwater barriers and mines that the Japanese had placed along the beaches where the marines would land.

The invasion was set for February 19. The marines and others who would be part of the invasion force ate a breakfast of steak and eggs. It not only tasted good, but would give them the energy they would need for the physical strain they were about to endure. But the men knew it was the last meal many of them would ever eat. Some were so nervous, they could not eat at all.

The Americans had stretched huge nets along the sides of some of the ships, forming giant rope

ladders. Marines used these to climb down into the Higgins boats that would take them to the island. A Higgins boat was 36 feet (11 meters) long, almost 11 feet (3 m) wide, and held thirty-six men. Other men were crammed into vessels called LVT's, or Landing Vehicle, Tracked. Also known as amtracks, these vessels could move through the water as boats, then crawl up onto land on tractor treads. They could carry twenty men or a small cannon and machine guns.

Marines on the deck of a ship bow their heads in prayer during a church service that was held the day before the invasion.

The American warships began a bombardment to destroy any Japanese troops that might be waiting on the beaches when the marines landed. Blasts of orange flame, rolling balls of smoke, and eardrum-shattering explosions erupted from the giant guns of the battleships. Shells rained down on the island, bursting with such force that Iwo Jima appeared to be shivering. It seemed to the watching sailors and marines that nothing could survive such a pounding.

But, once again, deep in their underground caves, the Japanese soldiers simply waited for the earth-shaking bombardment to end. When it did, they dashed through tunnels and scrambled up ladders into the hidden gun emplacements that faced the beach. There, they waited for the invasion.

Amtracks, several of them half-buried in the sand, carried the first cannons and machine guns onto the beach at Iwo Jima.

Troops come ashore from the open end of a troop carrier.

At 8:30 A.M. on February 19, hundreds of amtracks began moving through the water toward the island. The first to roll up onto the beach had cannons and machine guns to protect the unarmed troop carriers behind them. The troop carriers plowed through the water, their front ends opened. From these, the first wave of 1,200 marines poured out onto the beach in a long line that stretched for 2 miles (3 km). Marines fell as they were struck by Japanese bullets, and there was an occasional explosion of a mortar shell. But casualties (those who were dead or wounded) were surprisingly few. Many more vessels were coming through the water, bringing supplies, ammunition, trucks, tractors, tanks, and more troops. By the end of the first hour, there were thousands of marines on the beach and the invasion seemed to be going well.

Then, from the gun emplacements, the Japanese began firing. Bullets from dozens of machine guns hit the Americans crowding the beach. Mortar shells exploded among them. On Mount Suribachi, cannons fired shells down onto the beach. Many marines were horribly injured. Others were killed instantly. Shells were bursting among the landing craft heading for the shore. Within minutes, the beach and the water were littered with dead and wounded men, burning boats, and battered vehicles.

If the Americans on the beach tried to move forward they would continue to suffer casualties. But if they stayed where they were, they would be wiped out. There was no choice. They began to move forward slowly in small groups, writhing along flat on the ground like snakes, to avoid the bullets slicing through the air over their heads. A few amtracks and tanks moved forward with them, firing their cannons

Hauling carts of ammunition, the first wave of marines rushes onto the beach at Iwo Jima.

at anything that looked like it might be a gun emplacement. The sand was dotted with wide pits that had been made by the explosions of cannons and mortar shells. The men crawled from one to another of these, using them for protection.

Staying low to the ground, and taking cover in sand pits created by mortar shells, marines advance slowly across the beach.

Finally, groups of marines got close enough to enemy gun emplacements to fight back. Streams of fire from flamethrowers were squirted through the openings in the emplacements to kill the Japanese inside. Hand grenades were dropped in and exploded among the soldiers. One at a time, the gun emplacements were knocked out. The Americans continued to move slowly forward. By nightfall, men of the Fifth Division had made it all the way across the narrowest part of the island (about 700 yards, or 640 meters) to the opposite shore. They had cut off Mount Suribachi from the rest of the Japanese forces. But it cost the Americans 2,420 men (killed and wounded) of the thirty thousand that had landed.

Bodies of some of the marines who were killed during the invasion's first day

All night long, the Japanese continued to fire on the beach, and still more marines and sailors were injured and killed. Early on the morning of February 20, the marines again began to move forward. The Twenty-eighth Regiment of the Fifth Division turned south in order to capture Mount Suribachi and end the deadly artillery fire that was being hurled onto the beach. Once again, marines had to fight their way slowly through the gun emplacements. By the end of the day, they had gained only about 200 yards (183 m) and had suffered 152 casualties.

The rest of the regiments moved north to capture the two Japanese airfields, and then try to gain control of the rest of the island. But this was where General Kuribayashi had put his strongest defenses. Almost at once, the marines ran into an area of eight hundred machine gun, mortar, cannon, and antitank emplacements, hundreds of buried mines, and snipers. (Snipers are people

who fire at an enemy from hidden areas.) American tanks were knocked out when they ran over mines, or were blown open by direct hits from antitank guns. Marines were killed by machine gun fire and mortar bursts, or were hit by snipers' bullets. But here, too, flamethrower teams, grenades, and explosive charges destroyed the Japanese emplacements. Snipers were eliminated with rifle fire. A little at a time, the marines gained ground. By the day's end, they had advanced about 500 yards (183 m) and captured one of the airfields, but they had also suffered 351 casualties.

Among those who participated in the invasion were men of two of the U.S. Navy's Construction Battalions. Because of the initials of their unit— C. B.—they were known as the Seabees. Their motto was, "We can work and we can fight!" They were specially trained in construction work, and they were on Iwo Jima to repair the airfields after the invasion for use by American planes.

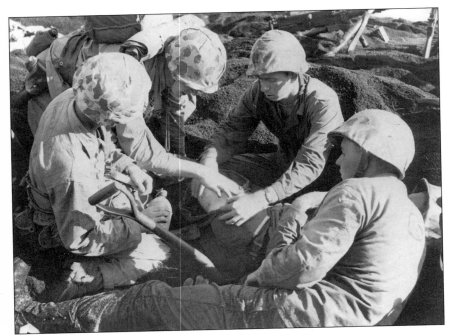

Corpsmen treat a marine who was wounded during the first week of the fighting.

There were also other sailors with the marines. They wore the same uniforms as marines, but did not carry any weapons. They carried packs filled with bandages, drugs and medicines, surgical instruments, and other first-aid materials. They belonged to the U.S. Navy Hospital Corps, and were known as Corpsmen. They were trained to do whatever they could to save the lives of the wounded— even if it meant risking their own lives to crawl through heavy fire to rescue an injured man.

Day three of the invasion (February 21) dawned. The Americans again pushed toward Mount Suribachi and the second airfield. The marines continued to crawl forward and suffer many casualties, but they destroyed the enemy defenses that were in their way. Meanwhile, thousands of more troops landed, as well as more cannons, ammunition, and tanks. There were now sixty thousand marines on Iwo Jima. The Japanese had lost any chance of pushing the Americans off the island.

But the Japanese would not surrender. Late in the afternoon, they struck at the American fleet. Planes flying from a distant island made kamikaze attacks on the ships lying off Iwo Jima. The word kamikaze means "divine wind." An attack consisted of crashing planes loaded with bombs directly into American ships, causing an explosion that might damage a ship so badly that it would sink. This would also kill the kamikaze pilot, but the Japanese pilots regarded it as an honor to die in an attempt to sink an enemy ship.

Most of the kamikaze planes were shot down by antiaircraft fire. But some reached their targets. One crashed into the deck of the aircraft carrier *Bismarck Sea*, erupting in a tremendous explosion. Three hours later the ship, with 218 sailors on board, sank.

In this photograph, taken during a kamikaze attack, a Japanese plane is just seconds away from crashing into the deck of an American aircraft carrier.

On the fourth day of the invasion (February 22), the American troops moving north were locked in a terrible struggle at the airfield. The marines had captured it twice, but were pushed back by the enemy. They suffered many casualties and were unable to move ahead.

However, the regiment pushing toward Mount Suribachi had reached the volcano's base and was starting to move up its slopes. The Americans were helped by a heavy rainstorm that kept the Japanese from seeing them well. Also, many of the Japanese soldiers defending Mount Suribachi had been killed during the marines' advance. There weren't many defenders left to stop them.

By 9:40 A.M. on February 23, marines were reaching the volcano's summit. One man carried a small American flag. Two marines

Troops fire missiles at Japanese gun emplacements in the struggle for control of the second airfield.

found a long piece of drain pipe, and the flag was attached to it. The end of the pipe was wedged into some rocks so the American flag could fly atop Mount Suribachi. Those watching from below and from ships near the beach could clearly see the flag, and knew Mount Suribachi had been captured. There were cheers and yells of triumph.

The marines who had raised the flag decided it should be preserved as a historical trophy, and looked for another flag to replace it. A much larger flag was donated by one of the vessels offshore. It was taken to the top of Mount Suribachi and fastened to another piece of drain pipe. Five marines and a navy corpsman lifted it upright. A marine photographer took motion pictures of the flag raising. A newspaper photographer snapped a photograph that would become famous.

This photograph, taken by newspaper reporter Joe Rosenthal, became one of the most recognizable pictures in U.S. history.

23

On the seventh day of the invasion (February 25), the second airfield was finally taken from the Japanese. American forces now held the entire southern half of Iwo Jima. Regiments of all three divisions were in a line across the middle of the island from one coast to the other.

On one side of the island, the Fifth Division entered an area of rocky ridges and deep gorges. In the center of the island, the Third Division moved beyond the airfield. On the other side of the island, the Fourth Division headed into an area that became known as "the meatgrinder," because of the way it "ground up" marines. It was a high, hilly region where the Japanese fired on the Americans from several directions. It took the Americans seven days to fight through the meatgrinder, and their casualties were high. The other divisions on the island continued to battle Japanese soldiers who refused to give up.

Marines in the meatgrinder take cover during an explosion of an enemy gun position.

As marines surround a destroyed enemy gun emplacement, a Japanese soldier is taken prisoner.

Fighting through Kuribayashi's toughest defenses, the three American divisions lost a total of thirteen thousand men.

On March 9, marines from the Third Division reached Iwo Jima's northern coast and saw the Pacific Ocean. This meant that almost the entire island was in American hands. Over the next few days, the last of the Japanese defenses were attacked. Despite the ferocious courage of the Japanese, the last of Kuribayashi's defenses were captured.

On March 16, twenty-six days after Iwo Jima had been invaded, General Schmidt declared Iwo Jima officially "secured," or captured. The Battle for Iwo Jima was over.

For days after, however, marines encountered Japanese soldiers who would not give up. There was no more fighting after March 26, but there were still hundreds of Japanese soldiers hiding in underground caves. Gradually, over many weeks—and in some cases, years—they surrendered.

For many people in the United States, the victory on Iwo Jima was the high point of the war against Japan. The motion pictures of the flag raising on Mount Suribachi were shown throughout the nation. The photograph taken by the newspaper reporter became the most famous photograph of World War II. For Americans, it symbolized the spirit of all those

The motto engraved on the United States Marine Corps War Memorial states, "Uncommon valor [courage in battle] was a common virtue."

who had served in the country's armed forces during the war. The photograph was printed in newspapers and magazines all over the United States. It inspired a popular song, "When the Yanks Raised the Stars and Stripes on Iwo Jima Isle." For a while, radio stations played this song almost every day. The photograph was featured on a U.S. postage stamp that was issued in July 1945, and again in 1995 to commemorate the fiftieth anniversary of the battle. It later served as a model for the

United States Marine Corps War Memorial near Arlington National Cemetery, in Virginia. The monument honors all of the marines who have died in combat since the Marine Corps was founded in 1775.

However, to gain the victory on Iwo Jima, the U.S. Marine Corps had more men killed and wounded than in any other battle in its history. The Japanese force of 20,000 men had mostly been destroyed, but the marines' casualties totaled more than 26,000. The navy's losses were close to 3,000, and the air corps and army troops also suffered losses. Some Americans questioned if such a costly, bloody victory had been worth it.

The United States Marine Corps Fourth Division Cemetery on Iwo Jima

The Americans who flew the bombers that pounded Japan every day thought so. Many planes were hit by antiaircraft fire, and were so badly damaged they couldn't make it back to their airbases. With no place to land, they would have had to crash into the sea. This would have meant certain death for many of the eleven-man bomber crews. But Iwo Jima under American control became an emergency landing field for bombers returning from Japan, and 2,400 planes

This photograph of fighter pilots, safely at the American base on Iwo Jima, was taken in April 1945.

carrying 27,000 crewmen made emergency landings there. A pilot who had to make several such landings declared, "Whenever I land on this island, I thank God—and the men who fought for it."

The Battle for Iwo Jima was the next-to-last battle of World War II. Within five months of Iwo Jima's capture, Japan surrendered and World War II was over.

Part of a huge crowd in New York's Times Square reacts to the news of Japan's surrender on August 14, 1945.

GLOSSARY

aircraft carrier

bombardment

aircraft carrier – warship with a large, flat deck where aircraft take off and land

antiaircraft gun – cannon designed for defense against air attack

barrage – heavy gunfire that occurs for a long time

battleship – warship armed with powerful guns

bombardment – an attack with heavy gunfire

concrete – building material made from a mixture of sand, gravel, cement, and water

cruiser – warship that was faster than a battleship and had smaller guns

defense – gun emplacement or other structure used to fight off attackers

destroyer – small, fast warship that used explosive devices called depth charges to protect other ships from attack by submarines

extinct – no longer active

fleet – group of warships under one command

fortress – place that is strengthened against attack

surrender – to give up or admit defeat

vessel – ship or large boat

TIMELINE

1939 *September 1:* World War II begins
in Europe

December 7: Japanese attack Pearl **1941**
Harbor, United States enters war

June 4–6: Battle of Midway **1942**

1944

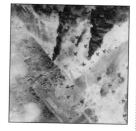

October 23–26:
Battle for Leyte Gulf

December 8: Bombing
raids on Iwo Jima begin

1945

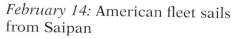

February 14: American fleet sails
from Saipan

February 16: American warships
surround Iwo Jima

February 19: Battle for Iwo Jima begins

February 20: Marines capture one airfield

February 21: Japanese begin kamikaze
attacks

February 22: Struggle continues for
second airfield, Americans reach base
of Mount Suribachi

February 23: U.S. flag raised on
Mount Suribachi

February 25: Second airfield captured,
marines enter "meatgrinder"

March 9: Marines reach Pacific Ocean

March 16: Battle for Iwo Jima ends

March 26: Final fight on Iwo Jima

August 14: Japan surrenders, World
War II ends

Mount Suribachi

DEDICATION

As a former Corpsman of the U.S. Navy Hospital Corps in World War II, I proudly dedicate this book to all Corpsmen who served on Iwo, and everywhere else.

INDEX (**Boldface** *page numbers indicate illustrations.*)

airfields (Iwo Jima), **6,** 7, 11, 18, 19, 20, 22, 24

amtrack, 13, **14,** 15, 16

Battle for Leyte Gulf, 6

Battle of Midway, 6

battleships, **4,** 5, 8, 12, 14

bombardments, 8, 10, 14

bombers (B-29), 6, 7, **7,** 28

Construction Battalions. *See* Seabees

Corpsmen, 20, **20,** 23

frogmen, 12

Guam, 4, 12

gun emplacements, 8, 11, 14, 16, 17, 18, 19, **22, 24, 25**

Iwo Jima, **6,** 7–10, 12, 14, **14, 16,** 19, 21, 24–29, **27**

Japan, 3, 4, 5, 6, 7, 26, 28, 29

kamikaze, 21, **21**

Landing Vehicle, Tracked. *See* amtrack

marines, 9, 10, 12–15, **13, 16,** 17–20, **17, 18, 19,** 22–27, **24, 25**

meatgrinder, 24, **24**

Mount Suribachi, 3, **6,** 8, 16, 18, 20, 22, 23, 26

Pacific Ocean, 3, 5, 25

Pearl Harbor, Hawaii, 4, **4**

Philippines, 4, 6

Saipan, 12

Schmidt, Harry, 10, **10,** 25

Seabees, 19

snipers, 18, 19

Sulfur Island. *See* Iwo Jima

Tadamichi Kuribayashi, 8, 9, 18, 25

troop carrier, 15, **15**

Turner, Richmond, 10, **10**

United States, 4, 5, 26

U.S. Army Air Corps, 10

U.S. Marine Corps War Memorial, **26,** 27

U.S. Navy, 6, 10, 12, 19, 20

U.S. Pacific Fleet, 4, 5

Wake Island, 4

World War II, 4, 26, 29

PHOTO CREDITS

Photographs ©: AP/Wide World Photos: cover, 1, 2, 6, 13, 14, 15, 18, 19, 23, 24, 25, 27, 31 top left, 31 bottom; Photri: 26; UPI/Corbis-Bettmann: 4, 5, 7, 8, 10, 11, 16, 17, 20, 21, 22, 28, 29, 30 top, 30 bottom, 31 top right; map: TJS Design.

ABOUT THE AUTHOR

Tom McGowen is a children's author with special interests in military history and the Old West. He lives in Norridge, Illinois, and is the author of forty-seven books for young readers, including *African-Americans in the Old West* (Cornerstones of Freedom). In 1990, Mr. McGowen won the Children's Reading Roundtable Award for Outstanding Contribution to the Field of Juvenile Literature.